Cotton is the yarn most often used for crochet but other types can occasionally be found. This one-ply mohair shawl was purchased in Germany at the end of the nineteenth century as a honeymoon gift.

CROCHET
A history of the craft since 1850

Pauline Turner

Shire Publications Ltd

CONTENTS

Set in 9 on 9 point Times roman and printed in Great Britain by C. I. Thomas & Sons (Haverfordwest) Ltd, Press Buildings, Merlins Bridge, Haverfordwest.

British Library Cataloguing in Publication Data
Turner, Pauline
  Crochet : a history of the craft since 1850. ——(Shire album; 126)
  1. Crocheting——History
  I. Title
  746.43'4'0904   TT820

ISBN 0-85263-697-0

ACKNOWLEDGEMENTS
  The author wishes to thank Miles Cummings, who took the majority of the photographs; Tracey; Emma Flitcroft; Mrs Gorst and Miss Bilbrough for permission to photograph the hair tidy and the mohair shawl; Gawthorpe Hall for the use of a study room and Mrs Allen of Leicester Museum and Jeremy Farrell of the Nottingham Museum of Costume and Textiles for their invaluable help. Photographs are acknowledged as follows: by gracious permission of Her Majesty the Queen, page 22; M. Bilbrough, page 1; the National Library of Scotland, pages 8, 9, 19; the Nottingham Museum of Costume and Textiles, pages 17, 18. The line drawings are by D. R. Darton.

An example of crochet made by Emma Flitcroft in 1979, worked in 80 cotton.

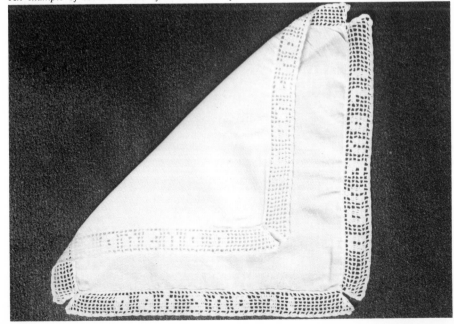

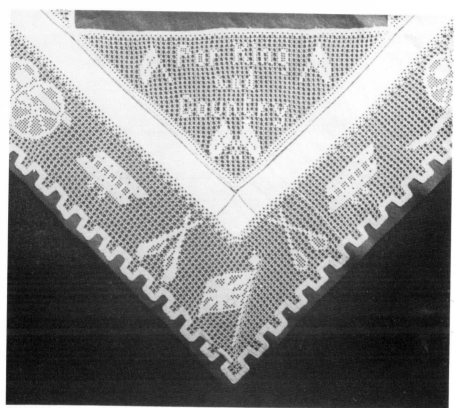

The corner of the crochet table-cloth edging shown on the front cover. The cloth was crocheted in England during the First World War. It depicts a gun carriage, biplane, crossed rifles, Union Jack, crossed swords and the motto 'For King and Country'.

INTRODUCTION TO CROCHET

The *Chambers Twentieth Century Dictionary* definition of crochet is 'looping work done with a small hook'. The word 'small' is unnecessary in the present day concept of crochet. Since 1970, when crochet developed new techniques and used different materials, the range of hook sizes has expanded greatly. Originally crochet used fine cottons in an attempt to copy the lace designs of traditional lacemaking. This work required small hooks with tiny barbed heads to manipulate the threads. This is not necessary in the 1980s when thick rug wool, string and even farmers' baler twine can be made into useful and beauti-

ful articles using crochet for their construction.

Crochet is a means of producing a textile using a hook which contains a single loop. No matter how complicated the crochet stitch construction, it will start with one loop on the hook and end with one on the hook in readiness for the next stage. To put the loop on the hook in the first place a slip knot is made. When following post-1970 crochet patterns the loops should be the circumference of the stem of the hook. As the hooks manufactured since that date have straight stems with an even diameter throughout, except near the barbed head, it is an easy

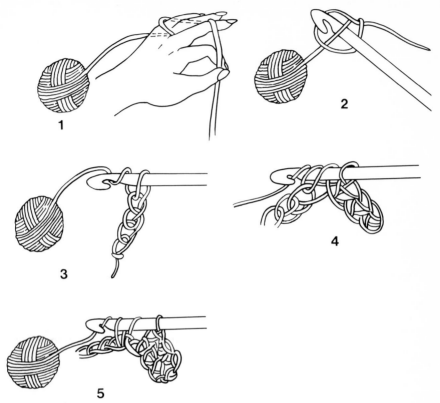

To work crochet:

1. Hold the yarn so that it flows smoothly and easily through the fingers. Hold the crochet hook as you would a pencil.

2. Make a slip knot by placing the end of a ball of yarn over the main length to form a loop and insert the hook as shown in the diagram. Pull the hook upwards as the thread from the ball of yarn and the tail end are pulled down together. Open the two threads so that the loop tightens on to the hook. All crochet begins and ends with a loop so this loop is not counted.

3. Most crochet needs a foundation chain to work from. To make a chain put the yarn over the hook ('y.o.h.'), dip the head of the hook under the thread lying between the index and middle fingers and pull through the loop that is already on the hook. This makes one chain.

4. All crochet instructions in the 1980s assume that two strands of the stitch will be picked up unless otherwise stated. To make a double crochet (UK terminology) insert the hook into the work, y.o.h., pull the thread through to the front of the work, y.o.h., pull the thread through the two loops on the hook to give only one loop. This makes one double crochet stitch. To work the next row, the first stitch must be a chain.

5. To make a treble put the yarn over the hook before inserting the hook into the work, y.o.h., and pull through to the front to give three loops on the hook (y.o.h. and pull the thread through two loops) twice, leaving one loop on the hook. A treble is a taller stitch than the double crochet and so the first stitch is made of three chains to turn the row back again.

NB. The chain, double crochet and treble stitches are the basic stitches of crochet. All other stitches are simply variations of these three.

rule to follow. However, the early hooks used the embroiderer's 'tambour' hook and this is shaped like a stylo with a fine hook on the end. The tension (the evenness of the looped stitches) had to be achieved by making certain that the loop under construction went to exactly the same point along the length of the hook every time.

There is much speculation over where and when crochet originated. As it is frequently linked with knitting, erroneous assumptions have been made that it is as old as knitting. If this were true and if (as seems likely) the craft of crochet started on the European continent it is strange that no paintings or writings describing crochet have been found — particularly as there are paintings of people knitting. There are many beautiful Renaissance paintings showing ladies making lace both with bobbins on a pillow and with the needle, but none showing them crocheting. A rare reference is in Mary Thomas's *Knitting Book*, where she describes the way the shepherds of Landes in southern France produced knitting using hooked needles made from umbrella ribs.

However, a textile which has been produced using only the 'hooked' fingers can not necessarily be classed as early crochet. Macramé and sprang use the fingers as tools to knot and loop threads together to form a fabric while crochet uses a hook. Some macramé and particularly sprang fabrics look like crochet but they have been worked with the fingers and should be disregarded as being crochet. The word 'crochet' came into the English language from the old French name for hook, *croc*. Ladies of the French nobility began writing on the subject of crochet from the mid nineteenth century, closely followed by those of Belgium and Spain. It was by young ladies educated in the convents on the continent that the craft was taken to Britain and America.

The following detailed crochet instructions, linked with the sketches of the hooks, yarn and stitches, should be sufficiently simple even for the reader who has never crocheted to attempt for herself.

HOW TO CROCHET
(from *The Enquirer's Home-Book*, 1910)
'Cotton, thread [presumably linen], wool or silk and a crochet-needle are the materials required for crochet work. The long wooden and bone crochet-needles are used for wool, while for cotton and silk short steel needles screwed into a bone handle are best. The beauty of crochet work largely depends upon the regularity of the stitches; they must be elastic, but if too loose they look as bad as if too tight. The work should be done only with the point of the needle; the stitch should never be moved up and down the needle.

All crochet work patterns are begun on a foundation chain. There are three kinds of foundation chains. The plain, the double, the purl. The plain foundation consists of chain stitches only.

Plain Foundation Chain — Form a loop with the cotton or other material with which you work, take it on the needle and hold the cotton, as for knitting, on the forefinger and other fingers of the left hand. The crochet needle is held in the right hand between the thumb and forefinger, as you hold a pen in writing; hold the end of the cotton of the loop between the thumb and forefinger of the left hand, wind the cotton once round the needle by drawing the needle underneath the cotton from left to right, catch the cotton with the hook of the needle and draw it as a loop through the loop already on the needle which is cast off the needle by this means and forms one chain stitch. The drawing of the cotton through the loop is repeated until the foundation chain has acquired sufficient length. When enough chain stitches have been made take the foundation chain between the thumb and forefinger of the left hand, so that these fingers are always close to and under the hook of the needle. Each stitch must be loose enough to allow the needle hook to pass easily through. All foundation chains are begun with a loop.

Double Foundation Chain — Crochet two chain stitches, insert needle downwards into the left side of the first chain stitch, throw cotton forward, draw it out as a loop, wind the cotton again round the needle and draw it through the two loops on the needle, *draw the cotton as

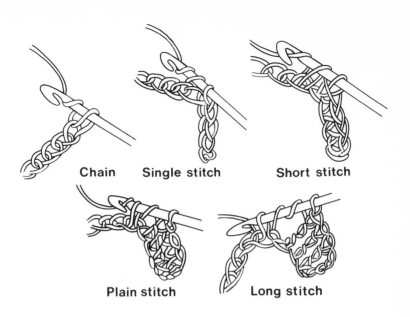

Chain **Single stitch** **Short stitch**

Plain stitch **Long stitch**

Stitches used in early crochet.

A SIMPLE EDGING IN FILET-STYLE CROCHET

1 block (blk) is made up of 3 trebles. 1 space (sp) is made of 2 chain (ch) and 1 treble (tr) with the treble worked into a treble. ss = slip stitch; st = stitch.

To make: work 29 ch.

1st row. 1 tr in 8th ch from hook, 6 tr, miss 2 ch, 1 tr in next ch, 3 tr, (2 ch, miss 2 ch, 1 tr in next ch) twice, 3 tr, 3 ch, turn.

2nd row. 1 blk, 2 sps, 1 blk, 1 sp, 2 blks, 1 sp, turn.

3rd row. ss across 3 sts, 5 ch, (miss 2 sts, 1 tr in next tr) twice, 5 blks, 5 ch, turn, miss 2 sts.

4th row. 1 tr in next tr, 3 sps, 3 blks, turn.

5th row. ss over 6 sts, 3 ch, 1 blk, 1 sp, 2 blks, 1 sp, 5 ch, turn.

6th row. 1 tr on next tr, 2 blks, 1 sp, 1 blk, 8 ch.

7th row. 1 tr in 4th ch from hook, 1 tr in each of 5 remaining chains, 1 blk, 4 sps, 3 ch, turn.

8th row. 5 blks, 2 sps, 7 ch, turn.

9th row. 1 tr on tr, 2 blks, 1 sp, 1 blk, 2 sps, 1 blk, 3 ch, turn.

Repeat rows 2-9 inclusive for the 8-row pattern.

When edging has reached the length required work 1 row double crochet along the squared edge for firmness.

The diagram (below) shows how this pattern is put on to graph paper. Using the same method it is possible for even those with little crochet experience to design simple edgings for themselves.

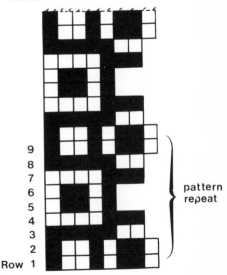

pattern repeat

Row 1 2 3 4 5 6 7 8 9

6

a loop through the left side of the last stitch, wind the cotton round the needle, and draw it through both loops on the needle. Repeat from * until the foundation chain is long enough.

Purl Foundation Chain — Crochet four chain stitches, then one treble stitch — that is wind the cotton round the needle, insert the needle downwards into the left side of the first of the four chain stitches, wind the cotton round the needle, draw it through the stitch, wind the cotton again round the needle and at the same time draw the cotton through the last loop and through the stitch formed by winding the cotton round the needle. Wind the cotton once more round the needle, and draw it through the two remaining loops on the needle. The four chain stitches form a kind of scallop or purl.

Slip Stitch — Draw the needle through the back part of a plain or double foundation chain stitch, or in the course of the work, through the back part of a stitch of the preceding row, wind the cotton round the needle, and draw it through the stitch and loop on the needle.

Double Stitch — Double stitches are worked nearly like slip stitches. Draw the cotton as a loop through the back part of a stitch, wind the cotton round the needle and draw it through the two loops on the needle.

The Ribbed Stitch — This stitch is worked backwards and forwards, that is, the right and wrong sides are worked together, which forms the raised ribs. Insert the needle always into the back part of every stitch. Work one chain stitch at the end of every row, which is not worked however in the following row.

Slanting Stitch — This stitch is worked like that described in the article headed Double Stitch. The cotton is not wound round the needle the first time in the usual manner, but the needle is placed through the back loop above the cotton. Draw the cotton through as a loop, the stitch is finished like the common double stitch.

Cross Stitch — This stitch is worked like "Slanting Stitch" on a foundation like the Double Foundation Chain, only insert the needle through the two upper sides of a stitch.'

It is interesting to see that the 'double foundation chain' and the 'purl foundation chain' are almost non-existent now. The 'ribbed stitch' reflects the crochet technique of that time by stressing the need to work this stitch in rows rather than in a round or a circle, which was more usual.

A CROCHET COSY COVER

In this cosy, a novel and pretty effect is gained by working a plain filet background of open meshes, and sewing the crocheted roses on to it.

To make the cosy cover, cut out a piece of paper 9 inches (23 cm) wide and 8 inches (20 cm) deep. Taper the top off to a point and work a plain piece of open mesh crochet to this shape, consisting of holes of 2 ch, 1 tr. The holes may be worked over one another or alternatively. Work three of these pieces and join together with loops of 15 ch. On each side, sew nine roses, one large three medium sized and five small. Work with Ardern's Number 40 Crochet Cotton. (dc = double crochet; ltr = long treble.)

The large rose

8 ch, join into a ring with a slip stitch, into this work 12 dc.

1st row. 5 ch, miss 1 dc, 1 dc in the next, work this all round, making in all 6 holes.

2nd row. 1 dc, 1 tr, 4 ltr, 1 tr, 1 dc into every loop, join with a slip stitch.

3rd row. 6 ch, 1 dc on dc between petals, make chain come behind petal, repeat all round.

4th row. 1 dc, 1 tr, 6 ltr, 1 tr, 1 dc in every loop, join as before.

5th row. 8 ch, 1 dc behind petal all round.

6th row. 1 dc, 1 tr, 8 ltr, 1 tr, 1 dc in every loop, join.

7th row. 10 ch, 1 dc behind every loop.

8th row. 1 dc, 1 tr, 10 ltr, 1 tr, 1 dc in every loop, join.

9th row. 11 ch, 1 dc behind every petal, join.

10th row. 1 dc, 1 tr, 12 ltr, 1 tr, 1 dc in every loop.

11th row. 12 ch, 1 dc behind every petal.

12th row. 1 dc, 1 tr, 14 ltr, 1 tr, 1 dc in every loop, join.

Slip up to fourth stitch of 1st petal. 7 ch, slip stitch into 5th ch from hook to form a picot, make 2 more picots, 2 ch, 1 dc into 4th tr from opposite side of same petal. Do this all round, making one loop of three picots over every petal and one in between every petal, join with a slip stitch to where first loop starts. Break off cotton and join to centre picot of first loop. Do 4 picots and join to centre picot of next loop, repeat all round, join at end as before and break off cotton. This completes large rose.

The medium sized rose

Work first four rows of large rose only, working tr instead of ltr, work 2 rows of picot loops round this, making two and three picots instead of three and four, as in large rose.

The small rose

1st two rows of medium rose, and only one row of picot loops. Sew on to the pieces of crochet work. Thread up with ribbon.

A STRONG IRISH EDGING FOR LINEN

1st row. 7 ch, and catch with a dc into the edge of the cloth. Repeat all round, allowing very little fullness for each loop, as they stand off in curves when the double crochet is added in the next row.

2nd row. Work over each loop of 7 ch below, *3 dc, 4 ch for the picot, 8 dc (close workers can get in 9 dc), catch into edge of cloth. Repeat from *.

3rd row. *7 ch, catch into centre of loop below. Repeat from *.

4th row. Like 2nd row.

5th row. Like 3rd row.

6th row. Into 1st loop work * 3 dc, 4 ch for picot, 6 dc, 4 ch for picot, 3 dc, catch into point below. Into next loop work 3 dc, 4 ch for picot, 3 dc, 7 ch, turn back and catch it into centre of dc in previous loop. Into this 7 ch work 3 dc, 4 ch for picot, 2 dc, 4 ch for picot. 2 dc, 4 ch for picot, 3 dc. This brings you back to the half-worked loop below, at point where you turned back. Now go straight on and complete the half-worked loop with 3 dc, 4 ch for picot, 3 dc, catch into point below. Repeat from *.

'Greek Lace' crochet from Mlle Riego de la Branchardiere's 'Crochet Book' (1863).

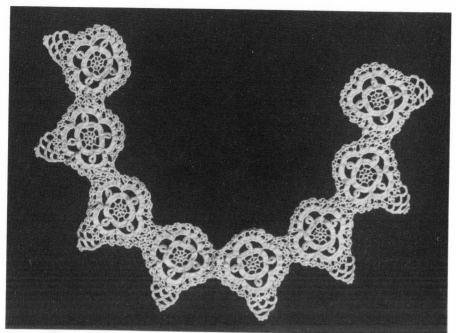

A part edging for a doily copying an embroidered lace design in filigree.

CROCHET'S CONNECTION WITH LACE

Crochet was not used in England much before 1850. Lace articles were still in demand for both fashion and household items but the cost of pillow, needle and embroidered laces was becoming exorbitant. The embroiderer's tambour hook was found to be an ideal tool for shaping fine cotton, linen or silk threads into fabrics to imitate the various lace designs which had been produced from the fifteenth century onwards. The tambour hook could produce a reasonable facsimile of these lace fabrics in less than a quarter of the time it took to make the same length of lace.

Lacemaking can be very loosely categorised into three main groups. The first two of these groups provided the type of pattern that could be imitated by the tambour hook:

1. Those made on pillows with bobbins and pins, such as the laces originating in Brussels, Genoa, Crete, Malta and Italy and British Honiton lace. Each area had its own individual style, which makes it possible to identify the place of origin of any piece of lace.

2. The group of laces known as needle-made lace which includes some of the more familiar names used to describe crochet patterns. For example, Reticella, Filet, Mignardaise and Venetian. English-point, Renaissance, Reticella and Mignardaise use hand-made braids to form the basis of their patterns. Crochet also copied the idea of using braids but used a machine-made version. The Reticella style is more geometrical than the simplified flower and leaf forms used in Renaissance lace. Some needle laces were applied to a net background and this idea was copied in crochet by making motifs with a hook and fine thread.

3. The elaborate embroidered laces were

LEFT: *Two samples of crochet insertion pieces.*
RIGHT: *Honiton lace designs. Note the similarity with the crochet, left.*

worked in self-colour on net or alternatively worked on linen using very rich lustre threads such as gold, silver and tinsel. The majority of the embroidered laces had a backing fabric but in the case of the Spanish filigree the backing was cut away to leave the embroidered lace free. Spanish lace is noted for its picots (loops of thread) and these have been carried through into many crochet patterns, for example the background to an Irish crochet.

By 1850 machine-made laces were available. Some of the braids, like the Mignardaise braid, had picot edges which made them ideal for inclusion in an openwork pattern. Using crochet thread and a hook, the picots could be used direct. Venetian lace was also copied to produce machine-made Guipure lace. Also by 1850 there were many people in Ireland copying the Venetian lace designs with fine linen and cotton threads to produce one of the best known styles of crochet — Irish crochet. This contains raised flowers with free-standing petals, leaves with the edges worked over a cord for padding and padded fruits while the whole item has a delicate network of chains and picots to connect the indi-

10

vidual motifs together.

Interest in the craft of crochet began in England, Wales and the Scottish lowlands between 1830 and 1840 as an extension to other types of needlecraft. Very little pre-1850 English crochet is to be found. The Irish, however, needed to produce crochet for their cottage industry as a subsidy or even a replacement for their income during the potato famine of 1845-7. Rachael Kay Shuttleworth, whose collection of needlecraft is one of the best in England and is housed at Gawthorpe Hall, Padiham, Lancashire, has written that 'the old Irish crochet lace was often lacking in design and cohesion but the background of chain and picots and the shell-petalled flowers often raised were all real craft with the hook'. In the rest of the British Isles crochet was an alternative to other needlecraft and generally copied the flatter lace designs. Filet in particular, with its blocks of solid work and its open spaces in the form of squares, was an easy lace to reproduce. Later, as printed patterns became available in larger quantities, filet crochet was found to be the simplest to describe. It was easy to obtain a clear photographic reproduction and simple to put into chart form. With three ways of presenting the design it was possible for anyone to copy it no matter how they had been brought up to produce crochet work. Because of its adaptability to graph paper, filet was used extensively to reproduce designs containing words and two-dimensional drawings. However, as Rachael Kay Shuttleworth commented, comparing filet needle lace with a crocheted copy: 'Filet lace has its beauty in the plain smooth effect and texture of darning on the netted squares which form a single

ABOVE: *This cuff edging for a day dress sleeve is also similar in design to one of the Honiton lace patterns opposite.*
BELOW: *Many of the embroidered laces had circles or part circles in their designs. This fine mat, c 1880, using 100 cotton, copies the delicacy of lace reasonably well.*

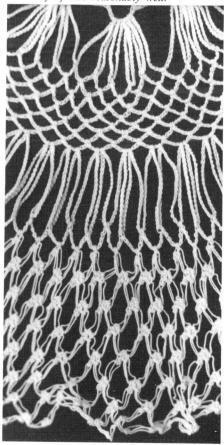

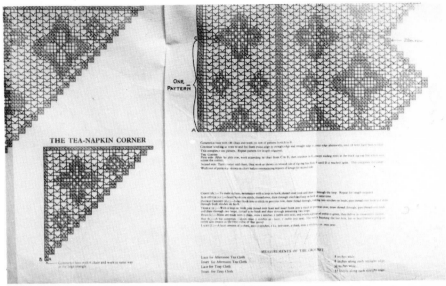

ABOVE: *A filet-style crocheted teacloth edging with corner insertions using a chart and written instruction. From a Weldon's Needle-Art Series journal.*

LEFT: *The Lord's Prayer is the latest design included in this period and was worked from a 'Pins and Needles' pattern. It shows how filet crochet is suitable for incorporating messages.*

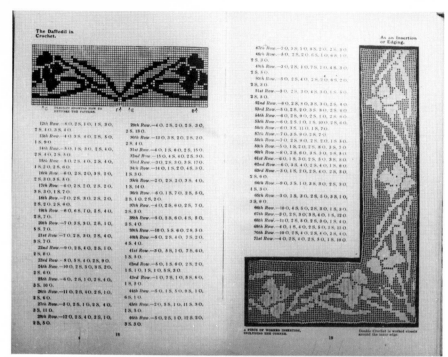

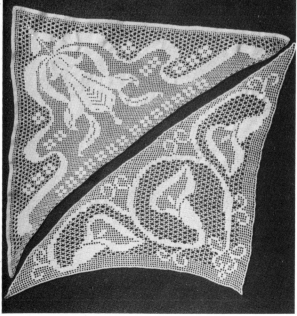

ABOVE: *A page from Flora Klickmann's book 'Beautiful Crochet on Household Linen'. This filet pattern uses the abbreviations S (solid), which is the same as a block of three trebles, and O (open), which is a space made by two chains and one treble.*

RIGHT: *Two corner insertions of different filet designs. Note the closeness of the pattern of the top corner piece, which was worked in 80 cotton, compared to the bottom corner insertion worked in 40 cotton.*

ABOVE: *A pattern for a guimpe using the Irish crochet motifs appliqued on to a net bodice pattern shape.*

LEFT: *A guimpe in filet crochet.*

thread basis with its essential knots at each corner of the mesh. This texture and this effect is unobtainable with a crochet hook and the flat smooth darned portions are replaced by ridges which form light and shade masses breaking up the surface'.

Another complaint about crochet work which attempted to copy lace was the coarseness of the thread that was so often used, particularly at the end of the nineteenth century and beginning of the twentieth. Presumably this was for speed but it did remove the delicate tracery effect of the finer laces. Although crochet copies were not as aesthetically pleasing as the real laces they did make lace effects available to a larger section of the population. Crochet had two derogatory nicknames, 'poor man's lace' and 'nun's lace', which reflect nineteenth-century prejudice against it.

Names were given to crochet designs rather than to the individual stitches, hence filet crochet was crochet in the style of filet lace. It also gave the crochet worker immediate information on how the crochet was done without it being laboriously explained that three trebles constituted one blocked-out square of a graph and two chain and one treble were represented by a plain square on the graph paper.

Besides copying lace designs, the crochet hook also imitated the designs produced with a tatting shuttle and a netting shuttle. One lady from Europe living in England, Mrs Cornelia Mee, introduced hairpin crochet in her *Manual of Needlework* (1856). This was an attempt to recreate more accurately the designs produced in the craft of netting. Another name for the hairpin was a *krotchee* and this name remained in use until the First World War. Even the art of macramé (knotting with the fingers) did not escape the insatiable desire of crochet workers to mimic anything and everything they could. The network of flat knots, known as 'Solomon's knots', in macramé is very similar to those stitches produced with a crochet hook and using the same name.

Even the ordinary stocking and garter stitches of knitwear failed to escape the onslaught of the crochet hook. What is commonly known in Britain as Tunisian crochet (and in America as Afghan crochet) was introduced to Britain as *tricot écossais* and produced a textile similar to knitted fabrics. The use of hooked knitting needles in areas such as Landes and Andorra and amongst the Berbers may be connected with this style of crochet. Mlle Eleanore Riego de la Branchardiere, an aristocratic lady who came to Great Britain during the early nineteenth century, claimed to have introduced this type of crochet to Britain in 1860. In America in 1859 a Mrs Pullman in her book *The Lady's Manual of Fancy Work* named the stitch 'Princess Frederick William Stitch'. Yet another name given to Tunisian crochet during the nineteenth century was *tricoter* and instructions for this type of crochet work were to be found in the *Lady's Crochet Book* by Mrs Jane Gaugain (1879).

A Victorian hair tidy. It was hung on a dresser, to collect hairs from comb or brush. Later this hair was used for stuffing pincushions, etc.

ABOVE: *A doily edging in crochet using solid crochet and open work to imitate Torchon lace patterns.*
BELOW: *A doily edging that copies in part the Sol lace designs.*

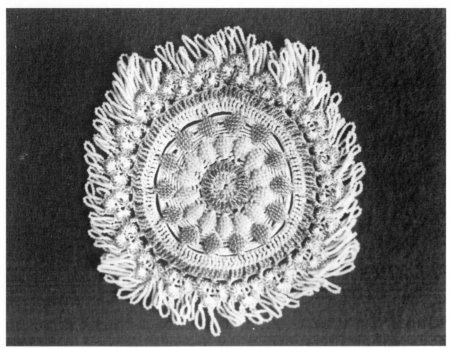

Mat, 1850-70, in white cotton with pale blue and clear yellow glass beads.

EARLY STITCHES AND DESIGNS

Initially the names of the stitches were often translations from European languages, particularly French. This was largely due to Mrs Gaugain and Mlle Riego. 'Crochet en air' was a term used to distinguish the textile from tambour embroidery. Both used a tambour style of hook. However, while tambour embroidery produced a design composed entirely of chain stitches which were anchored through a piece of fabric, 'crochet en air' produced the chain stitches free from any other material but also attached to those chain stitches previously made. The British term for this is 'single crochet'. After 1880 the use of this variation of a slip stitch as a stitch in its own right was rare. However, it is still used to give solidity to such items as pence jugs, long purses and beaded crochet mats.

Mrs Gaugain called all her crochet work by the embroidery term 'tambour', but all the main writers of the mid

nineteenth century, when writing about crochet work and its designs, used different terminology for the same process. This problem persisted for a century. By 1950 the names of the basic stitches printed in patterns within the United Kingdom had been standardised, as had their abbreviations, but a high proportion of other English speaking countries still use different names for the basic stitches. Many crochet patterns come into Great Britain from other countries and unless the crochet worker is aware of the difference in terminology the pattern will turn out quite differently from that expected.

There was a wide variety in crochet designs in the mid nineteenth century although the number of stitches used was small. The names of the stitches did not matter as the instructions were rarely given. The patterns were usually copied from charts or from actual crocheted samples. Those books written between

1850 and 1880 with patterns given in words were all accompanied by clear illustrations showing the stitches in detail either by sketch or by chart.

To illustrate this point there follows a selection of extracts from crochet pattern instruction books written between 1860 and 1875, with modern terms added. 'All tambour crochet should be worked rather loose than otherwise, as it is apt to cut when tight . . . great care should be taken in having the needle properly gauged according to the size of the receipts [pattern instructions] . . . Tambour dice bag in diamonds of blue and black [uses] the double tambour [double crochet] stitch'. (Mrs Gaugain's pattern).

In the *Winter Book* by Mlle Riego (1862) the names of the stitches differ from those above but because of the large volume of patterns that Mlle Riego produced she had a larger vocabulary of terms. These are listed here, again with the modern terms. 'Single crochet' or 'shepherd's knitting' is a slip stitch picking up one strand of the work only and giving a very stiff finish to the crochet fabric produced. 'Plain crochet' is a

LEFT: *Purse, mid nineteenth century, in brown, blue and cream silk with steel beads and steel fastening.*
RIGHT: *Small bag or purse, mid nineteenth century, in green, red and yellow silk with steel frame, handle and fringe.*

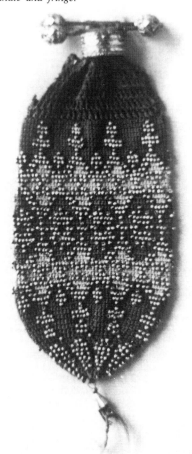

A sketch of a child's crochet lace frock which was incorporated in Mrs Rivers Turnbull's book 'Selected Works of Mlle Riego' (1903). The design originally dates from 1863-5.

double crochet in British terminology (single crochet in American). It picked up only one loop during this period instead of the two strands being picked up by the hook since 1950. A large proportion of crochet is worked in tubes or circles. To get the same effect working in rows it would be necessary to pick up the back loop on one row and the front loop on the next. 'Raised crochet' is as the 'plain crochet' except that the work is turned on every round to produce an elasticated fabric. 'Treble' is treble in post-1970 British terminology (double crochet in American). 'Long stitch' is the

British double treble or the American treble. 'Extra long stitch' was a term used to instruct the worker to wrap the yarn three or more times before inserting the hook into the work.

In the later books produced by Mlle Riego the 'double crochet' is introduced and she uses it to mean inserting the hook under two threads without having first wrapped the yarn round the hook. The term 'raised crochet' has also changed meaning. As Mlle Riego uses the term, the double crochet stitches were worked over a cord, as on the final row of an Irish crochet motif. Since 1970 'raised crochet'

A page from a book of patterns stitched on to blotting paper. Because of its frailty it cannot be on public view.

means picking up the lower part of a whole stitch by inserting the hook from front to back around the stem part of the stitch to emerge at the front, thus raising the stitch.

My Crochet Sampler by Miss Lambert uses the following unusual terms: plain, plain single crochet, plain double crochet, double stitch crochet, plain stitch elastic crochet, plain stitch open crochet, open crochet, double open crochet and treble open crochet. To the uninitiated, open crochet is a stitch followed by one chain. Yet treble open crochet is not one treble followed by one chain but three treble followed by one chain. To confuse the matter further, the plain stitch open crochet was five chains and one double crochet, while in her *Court Crochet Doyley Book* Mrs Warren

refers to the British treble (American double crochet) as a long stitch. Before the end of the First World War the British double crochet was frequently referred to as the short stitch, the British treble as the crochet stitch and the British double treble as the long stitch. These examples show clearly the lack of logic and uniformity in writing crochet patterns. This was an important factor in the decline of the craft.

The ninth edition of the *Encyclopaedia Britannica*, published in 1882, was the first to include a reference to crochet, but it was found under the heading of 'Knitting': 'Crochet is an analogous art differing from knitting in the fact that separate loops are thrown off and finished successively — whereas in knitting the whole series of loops go to form one length or round of the fabric and are retained on one or more needles while a series is being formed from them on a separate needle.' It gives as references Mrs Gaugain's *Knitting and Crochet Work* and Esther Copley's *Comprehensive Knitting Book*.

The eleventh edition of the Encyclopaedia (1910) retained a reference to knitting but excluded any information concerning crochet. By the fifteenth edition, it had transferred the section on knitting to 'Textile Industry' and once again there is no reference to crochet. There is also a complete omission of the works of Mlle Riego. Yet from 1846 to 1887 she wrote over a hundred books on knitting, tatting, crochet and lacework.

Mlle Riego also exhibited at the Great Exhibition during 1851 and received the only medal judged for crochet and point lace. Although there were not many entries in the crochet section, contemporary accounts suggest that her work deserved the award. Exhibitors in the Great Exhibition of 1851 under the section 'Crochet Work' were: Constable, Copeland, Cross, Danbt C. and T., Faudel and Phillips, Fryer, Irish Work Society, Lockwood, Podwick, Pearse, Riego de la Branchardiere, Sutton, Waterhouse E. and M., Woolcock, and Wratislow. The majority of the exhibits came from central and southern England with single exhibits from Ireland and Liverpool and two from Yorkshire. It may be, there-

20

A double page from a communal pattern book. Each worked pattern is stitched on to oiled cloth. From the variety of designs visible on these and other pages it would appear that this book was in use about 1900 but also very many years earlier.

fore, that crochet was not as widespread as it is sometimes quoted as being.

Even by 1850 most working-class women could not read and write though young ladies in the middle and upper classes were becoming accomplished in these skills. Nevertheless, needlecraft skills were usually handed down to them by their governesses, maiden aunts, mothers or elder sisters. Girls were shown how, and not left to read and decipher instructions for themselves. This was an important factor in creating much of the confusion still existing within the craft — even in the terminology and patterns of the post-1950 period. In hamlets, villages and small urban communities, there was often a communal pattern book which contained actual samples of crochet designs. Should someone within that community discover or invent a different pattern she would make an extra piece and add it to the cloth pages before passing it to the next person wanting to use the crochet 'pattern' book. It was not until after 1960 that crochet began to experiment with different yarns, hook insertions and many other techniques. Hence throughout the period 1850-1950 the stitches remained few and were easily copied.

The earliest record in the royal archives of any member of the royal family taking an active interest in crochet is this photograph, dated 1889, of Queen Victoria working with a tricot hook. Later Queen Mary, whose skill as a needlewoman is well known, also did crochet work.

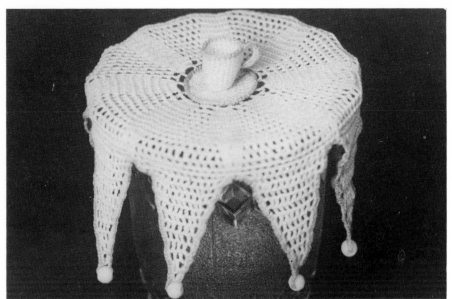

A beaded sugar basin cover in simple crochet stitches of blocks and spaces. The centre is a crocheted cup and saucer using the stiffer type of crochet called single crochet (a term now obsolete in the United Kingdom).

THE CHANGING TIMES

From the communal sample pattern books and the often vague and confusing early printed crochet instructions of the mid to late nineteenth century, crochet patterns became much more precise. In addition common abbreviations began to appear for the stitches in use at the end of the nineteenth century.

Three factors influenced the dramatic change in crochet. Firstly, in middle-class homes there were fewer servants, so that the ladies of the house were no longer free from all household duties. Secondly, it was the fashion during the Victorian era to have covers for practically every piece of furniture. Thirdly, it was believed in the late nineteenth century that the royal household were prolific crocheters. In that period if something could be connected with the royal household it had an air of respectability that it might otherwise not have had.

It has been a persistent belief that Queen Victoria and her sisters were taught to crochet at a very early age and that the British royal family produced much crochet. These assumptions seem to have arisen from the following passage of a letter, written on 7th March 1887 by Mlle Riego to a friend and published in *Selected Works of Mlle Riego on Crochet, Knitting, Lacework*, by Mrs Rivers Turnbull (1904): 'It seems strange to me to be again designing for the Court. My first knitting was for the Queen's (her late Majesty's) Mother, the Duchess of Kent; after teaching all her grand-daughters, and writing over one hundred books, I am able to make her Daughter's Jubilee lace'. This passage encouraged the idea that Mlle Riego might have taught crochet to the royal household. Since most of Mlle Riego's books were on crochet it was assumed that crochet was what she taught, rather than knitting. However, the royal archives have no record of Mlle Riego teaching anyone in the royal household to crochet, and the earliest record they have is of Queen Victoria crocheting in 1889 using a tricot (Tunisian) hook.

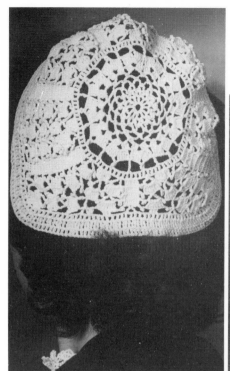

BELOW: *A Victorian mat, probably used as a 'throw-over' to prevent dust settling on food. The crocheted edging is wholly of chains and slip stitches, to copy the style of netted lace.*

ABOVE: *A Victorian baby's bonnet worked in 40 cotton.*

RIGHT: *A beautiful example of mid nineteenth-century Irish crochet.*

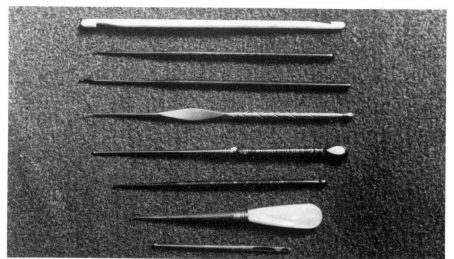

In the mid nineteenth century hooks were mostly hand-made from bone or metal. The metal could be brass, steel (not stainless), copper, etc. The ends of the hooks were often ornamented by etching, carving or other embellishments.

EQUIPMENT AND MATERIALS 1900-14

There were many thicknesses, types and brands of cotton threads on the market at the start of the twentieth century, of which the following are just a few: Strutts Crochet Cotton Number 36, Arden's Crochet Cotton Number 20, Penelope Cable Twist Number 30, Peri Lusta Crochet Cotton Number 24, Briggs' Crochet Silk, Harris Crochet Cotton, Hedebo Mercerised Cotton, Evan Number 18 Crochet Cotton, DMC and Coats Mercerised Cotton. DMC and Coats are still available, unlike most of the other brands of that time. J. and P. Coats produced cottons varying in thickness from number 3 to 100, the latter being the finest. Cotton was the most commonly used fibre for crocheting, but linen and silk threads were also used. Some fine botany wool was worked for articles of dress.

At the start of the twentieth century the types of crochet hook were numerous. Most of these were made from steel and used a special hook gauge ranging from 0 to 7½, with half sizes throughout the range. The highest number on the gauge is for the smallest hook head. In addition there were many beautiful hand-made hooks from before the First World War and these have now become collector's items. The larger hooks were made in bone or wood with the bone in particular having a hook head at each end. Unlike the later double-ended Tunisian hooks, which have the same size hook head at each end of a long shaft or stem, the bone hooks had a different size head at each end of a short shaft. This one hook with two sizes of head was used for any thickness of wool. The crochet worker varied the spacing of the stitches by judging how far along the shaft or stem she had to push the wool. The earliest tricot or Tunisian hooks were shorter than those in the post-1950 period and, like the crochet hooks, were made of either bone or steel.

Simple hairpins were used to make one kind of crochet 'lace'. The first experiments in using wider pronged hairpins were made by bending a double-ended steel knitting pin into a U shape. Another method was to slot two knitting needles with thin flat stop ends into a bar of wood. The bar had evenly spaced coun-

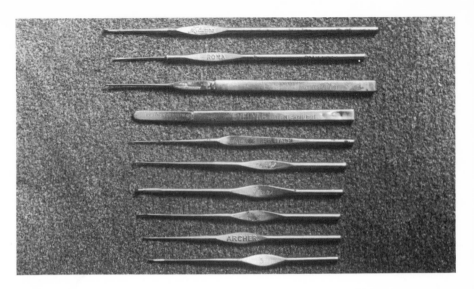

ABOVE: *Around 1900 there were almost as many makes of hooks as there were makes of cotton. From top to bottom these are: Milward, Roma, Evelyn (open), Evelyn (shut), Racket, Shield, Stari, Service, Archer and Venus.*

BELOW: *Number 13 of 'Needlecraft', an earlier journal than 'Fancy Needlework'. It usually concentrated on just one craft.*

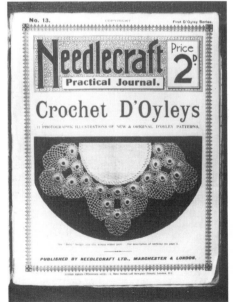

tersunk holes into which the knitting needles were slotted, enabling the space between the needles to be varied, not unlike the 'Quad' frame available in the 1870s. The wooden bar containing the knitting needles was clamped to the table but as this made the parallel sides on which the crochet was worked immovable it proved to be unwieldy and was not often used.

With the improvement of machines in the printing industry, journals such as *Needlecraft* and *Weldon's Practical Needlework* series became more readily available throughout Great Britain. These were priced at 2d for between twenty and thirty illustrated pages. The traditional brevity of instructions meant the crochet worker had to use imagination and common sense with no preconceived idea of how the article ought to look. With printed instructions there was a complete reversal in presentation. The explanations for the actions of the crochet hook became miniature essays. Common names for stitches and the positioning of the thread were all explained without any form of abbreviation either for the stitch names or the processes involved. This was often more difficult to follow than the previous type of crochet instruction and resulted in crochet still being made by copying the actual sample or article.

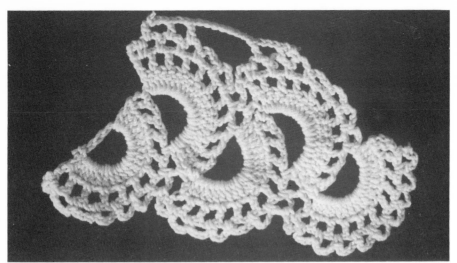

The 'crescent border' from Weldon's which was described in great detail using no abbreviations — almost an essay in itself.

By the twentieth century more items were being made by machinery. With such a wide choice of threads on the market the different manufacturers competed fiercely for a share in the home crochet market. Arden's put wider ball bands on their balls of cotton, advertising the quarterly *Fancy Needlework*. The inside of the ball band gave four illustrations of crochet patterns using their cotton. Because crochet designs were still simple the majority of crocheters buying the cotton could copy the design direct from the printed picture without having to buy the journal.

Another way to attract custom was for a manufacturer to pay a home-worker to crochet samples of their designs. These were then sold with the cotton bought to make it. The purchaser would continue from the sample which ensured the tension was correct before proceeding with the whole length. Crochet hook sizes were not specified. As crochet is extremely easy to pull back and creates no waste thread it did not matter how many times a continuation of the sample piece was practised. The worst that could happen was that it could become soiled. The most popular sample pieces to be purchased were those including a crocheted corner as this meant that square and rectangular cloths could have attractive edgings of crochet 'lace' added.

Tricot hooks — two in bone and one in steel. These hooks are now known as Tunisian or Afghan hooks. The centre one is similar to the hook Queen Victoria is using in the photograph on page 22.

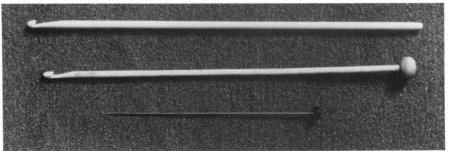

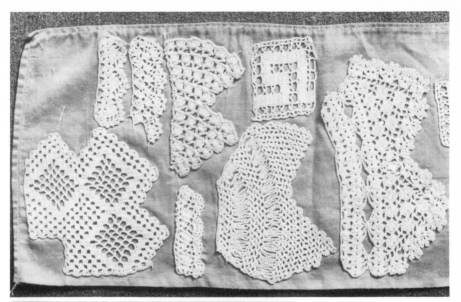

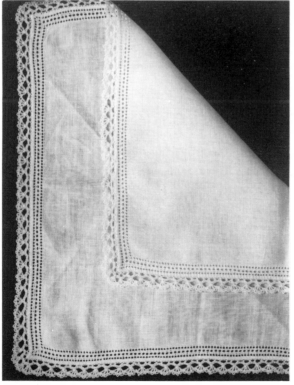

ABOVE: *A selection of crochet patterns purchased as samples and frequently incorporating a corner. Some of the examples shown here have had a second or third repeat worked, presumably by the purchaser, to ensure correct tension.*

LEFT: *Crocheted for the author by Emma Flitcroft. Worked in 100 cotton which she still had in her workbox from her childhood days.*

28

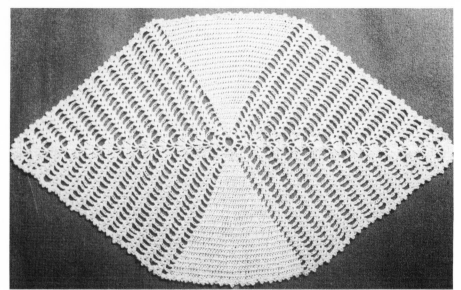

An 'art silk' mat with unimaginative stitching which has not held its shape well. Use of artificial silk (the name given to early viscose rayon) came after the First World War. It seems to have been used mostly during the period when little crochet was worked and did not encourage others to learn the craft.

FROM 1914 TO THE PRESENT

During the First World War crochet was produced in particular by those girls who were betrothed. They filled their 'bottom drawer' with household linen, such as pillowcases, tablecloths and covers, that had been edged in crochet. 100 but not 150 cotton was available, and as it was fine it was possible to edge handkerchiefs with delicate and intricate patterns. Sweethearts separated from their loved ones often crocheted messages around the edges of handkerchiefs using the filet crochet technique (blocks and squares on graph paper). The most popular version was a handkerchief to be carried by the young man in his breast pocket with the message 'I love you' crocheted on three sides and the name of his love on the fourth. There was little time for the young wife to do much more with her crochet than on a utilitarian basis such as hug-me-tight bodices, shawls, baby and children's clothes. The sewing machine took the place of the tapestry frame. Apart from those reserved for best, petticoats lost their lace edgings.

The shortage and increased cost of paper was partly responsible for a shorthand system being developed in crochet patterns. Abbreviations were introduced for basic stitches and the long drawn-out explanations of stitch processes were condensed. Printed patterns for woollen garments such as shawls, scarves, hats, gloves, mittens and slippers were introduced, but cotton crochet still predominated.

Some of the techniques of working Irish crochet changed around this time. Previously each motif had its final row worked over a thick cord, or groups of thinner threads, but this was beginning to be omitted, presumably for speed and economy. Traditionally motifs were placed individually and asymmetrically on to a prepared shape of paper or cloth and secured in position. The background was then worked by filling in the remaining spaces and at the same time connecting the motifs. Now Irish crochet introduced a design using squares, the centres of which had a 'traditional' Irish rose

29

motif while the background was still the chains and picots. The squares were then connected to form garments or household items.

During the First World War the use of the filet style increased while other crochet designs declined. This was partly because the crochet worker did not have to learn new techniques and it was easy to copy from a sketch, and partly because it took little space to write down in words.

Although crochet trims for undergarments were disappearing collars still remained fashionable, frequently adorning plainer items of dress. They had the advantage that they could be used on many outfits.

Another advantage with the filet style of crochet is that an error is soon apparent and swiftly rectified. With the coming of peace people were being forced to change their attitudes and some of their habits. Crochet was no longer an expected and routine part of the day. There was neither the time nor money to make non-essentials such as lace edgings. In addition there were enough items being handed down to children to last them through their lives, particularly as the mercerised cotton used on most household linen was extremely durable and could be washed frequently without coming to any harm. Fashions too had changed dramatically. The short hemlines of the 1920s were an indication that there was less money available to be spent on fabric and lace trimmings. Women no longer wanted to spend all their time in the home, and crochet lost its popularity. It was not until the 1970s that crochet regained a favourable place in the craft world.

With the decline in the use of cotton for craftwork and needlework many manufacturers went out of business. Those that remained had to select carefully the lines to produce. Between the two world wars the thickness of crochet cotton available became standardised into multiples of ten for any thickness over 10. Later the intermediate numbers were removed and cotton was only produced in multiples of twenty above 20. Eventually the extreme ends of the range, the 100 and 3, also disappeared. By the 1980s nothing finer than a 60 cotton was being produced although a tatting cotton of 70-80 was available. However, 5 and 8 softer cotton was revived for summer tops.

Larger sizes of hooks were made in plastic or composite material as well as in aluminium. Although hooks were available up to size 7mm (old size 2 wool) they were not extensively used. However they did eventually open the way to new and exciting crochet techniques which revived the art of crochet. With metrication in Britain in the 1970s, the sizes of hook changed from British Imperial to the Standard International sizes. Comparisons are given overleaf as there are many beautiful old patterns to be copied once the equivalent hook size is known.

ABOVE: *A circular mat in one of the pineapple designs of the early twentieth century. It was crocheted in the 1960s using Coats Number 10 mercerised red cotton. Pineapple designs were a copy of the Reticella lace designs.*

BELOW: *Short crochet gloves were popular, particularly for church attendance on Sundays. Note the simplicity of design and stitch usage.*

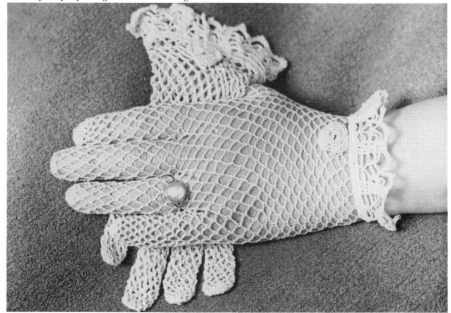

| | HOOK SIZES | | | |
| British Imperial | | Standard International | American | |
Wool	Cotton		Wool	Cotton
	7½			
	7	0.60		14
	6½	0.75		13
	6	—		12
	5½	1.00		11
	5	—		10
	4½	1.25		9
	4	—		8
16	3½	1.50		7
	3	—		
15	2½	1.75		6
	2	—	A	5
14	1½	2.00	B	4
		—		3
13	1	—	C	2
12	0	2.50	D	1
11	2/0	—	E	0
10	3/0	3.00	F	2/0
9		3.50	G	
8		4.00	H	
7		4.50	I	
6		5.00	J	
5		5.50		
4		6.00		
3		6.50		
2		7.00	K	
1		—		
0		8.00		
00		9.00		
000		10.00		
		12.00		

PLACES TO VISIT

The Crochet Design Centre, White Cross, Lancaster LA1 4XH. Telephone: Lancaster (0524) 33309.

The Gallery of English Costume, Platt Fields, Rusholme, Manchester M14 5LL. Telephone: 061-224 5217.

Gawthorpe Hall, Padiham, near Burnley, Lancashire BB12 8UA. Telephone: Burnley (0282) 78511.

Museum of Costume and Textiles, 51 Castle Gate, Nottingham NG1 6AF. Telephone: Nottingham (0602) 411881.

Old House Museum, Cunningham Place, Bakewell, Derbyshire. Telephone: Bakewell (062 981) 3647.

Victoria and Albert Museum, Cromwell Road, South Kensington, London SW7 2RL. Telephone: 01-589 6371.

Wygston's House Museum of Costume, 12 Applegate, Leicester. Telephone: Leicester (0533) 554100, extension 213.